Learn to Code

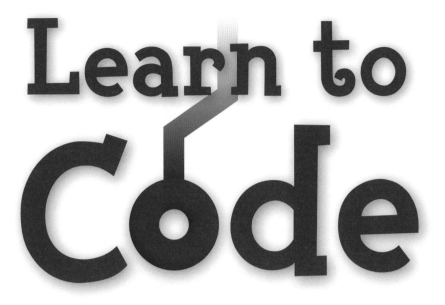

Practice Book 4

Written by

Claire Lotriet

Published by

RISING ★ STARS

Rising Stars UK Ltd, 7 Hatchers Mews, Bermondsey Street, London SE1 3GS
www.risingstars-uk.com

Published 2015

Author: Claire Lotriet
Computing consultant: Miles Berry
Text design: Words and Pictures Ltd, London
Typesetting: Words and Pictures Ltd, London
Cover design: Burville-Riley Partnership
Publisher: Becca Law
Editorial: Jenny Draine
Project manager: Estelle Lloyd
Illustrations: Eva Sassin, Advocate Art

Photo acknowledgements: pages 8–10, 12–14, 16–18, 20–22: screenshots from
TouchDevelop https://www.touchdevelop.com TouchDevelop is a Microsoft Research
project; pages 24–26, 28–30, 32–34, 36–38: screenshots from AppInventor http://
appinventor.mit.edu licensed under Creative Commons licence; pages 40–42, 44–46,
48–50, 52–54: screenshots from https://www.python.org copyright © 2001–2014 Python
Software Foundation; all rights reserved. All used with permission.

Rising Stars is grateful for the following people and their schools who contributed to
the development of these materials: Matt Rogers, Snowsfields Primary School; Dawn
Hallybone, Oakdale Junior School; Marc Faulder, Burton Joyce Primary School; Martyn
Soulsby, North Lakes School; John Janowski, Royal Russell Junior School.

British Library Cataloguing in Publication Data.
A CIP record for this book is available from the British Library.

ISBN: 978-1-78339-344-2

Printed by Newnorth Ltd, Bedford

Contents

How to use this book

Learning to code can seem like learning a new language! This book will show you how to code using three different tools. You will make your own apps and Python programs!

The step-by-step instructions explain what you need to do.

This text shows what you need to type in.

This text shows the commands you need to use in the program.

This text shows the words you'll see on the screen.

Handy tips give you extra help.

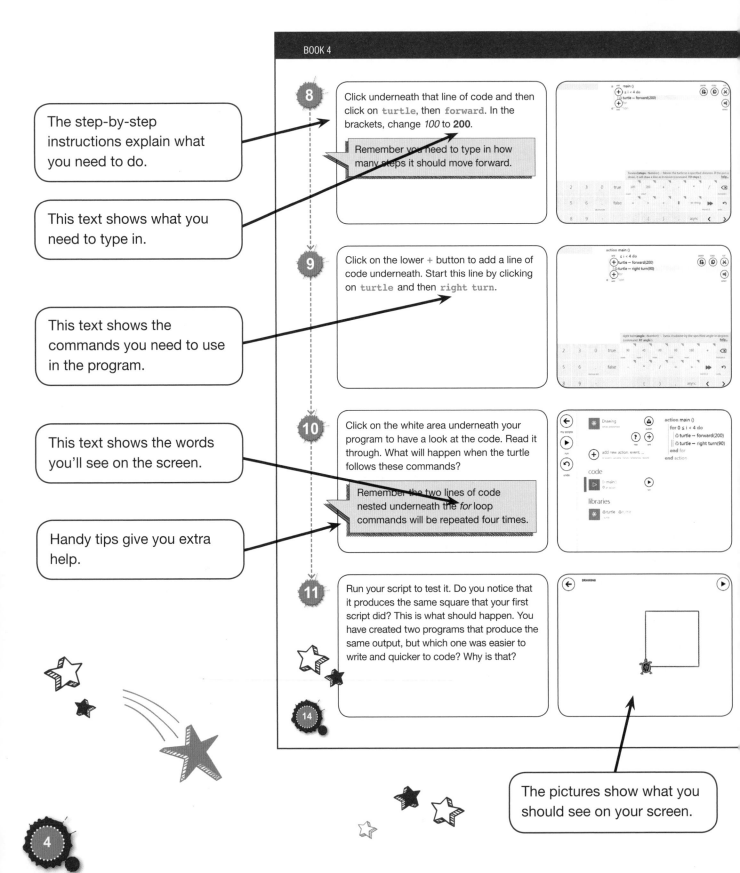

BOOK 4

8 Click underneath that line of code and then click on turtle, then forward. In the brackets, change *100* to **200**.

> Remember you need to type in how many steps it should move forward.

9 Click on the lower + button to add a line of code underneath. Start this line by clicking on turtle and then right turn.

10 Click on the white area underneath your program to have a look at the code. Read it through. What will happen when the turtle follows these commands?

> Remember the two lines of code nested underneath the *for* loop commands will be repeated four times.

11 Run your script to test it. Do you notice that it produces the same square that your first script did? This is what should happen. You have created two programs that produce the same output, but which one was easier to write and quicker to code? Why is that?

14

The pictures show what you should see on your screen.

4

This book uses three tools: TouchDevelop, App Inventor and Python. Work your way through the activities for each tool in order. Each activity builds on what you have learned in the previous one.

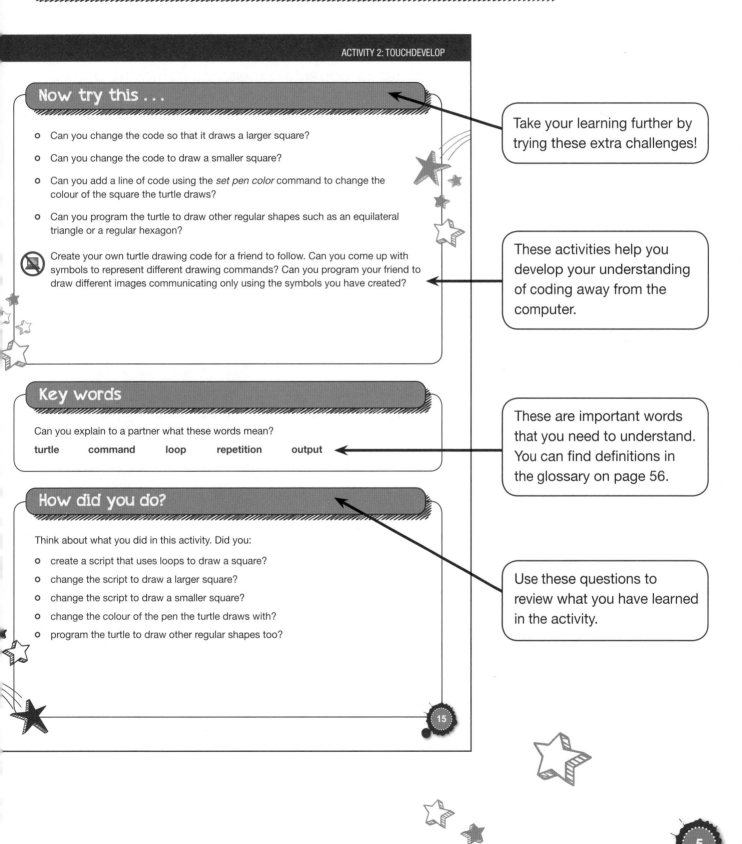

Now try this . . .

- Can you change the code so that it draws a larger square?

- Can you change the code to draw a smaller square?

- Can you add a line of code using the *set pen color* command to change the colour of the square the turtle draws?

- Can you program the turtle to draw other regular shapes such as an equilateral triangle or a regular hexagon?

Create your own turtle drawing code for a friend to follow. Can you come up with symbols to represent different drawing commands? Can you program your friend to draw different images communicating only using the symbols you have created?

Take your learning further by trying these extra challenges!

These activities help you develop your understanding of coding away from the computer.

Key words

Can you explain to a partner what these words mean?

turtle   **command**   **loop**   **repetition**   **output**

These are important words that you need to understand. You can find definitions in the glossary on page 56.

How did you do?

Think about what you did in this activity. Did you:

- create a script that uses loops to draw a square?
- change the script to draw a larger square?
- change the script to draw a smaller square?
- change the colour of the pen the turtle draws with?
- program the turtle to draw other regular shapes too?

Use these questions to review what you have learned in the activity.

15

Top tips

Writing code to make something happen is exciting, but sometimes your code won't work as well as it could, or it won't work at all!

What happens when your code doesn't do what you want it to? You need to fix it!

The process of making our code better, or correcting mistakes (removing bugs in the code) is called debugging.

If you find a problem with your code, try to solve it yourself first, before asking a grown-up. The coding monsters are here to help you!

Ask a grown-up to help you find an image of a rolling dice and a sound effect for activity 5.

When you have finished writing your code, always run your program or script to see if it works.

Go through your code step by step in your head. Try to predict what will happen. Can you spot any mistakes?

for coding

Try explaining each bit of your code to a partner. Does it all make sense?

Try explaining your code to a rubber duck. Rubber duck debugging is used by proper programmers to fix errors in their code!

Show your code to a partner. Do they have any ideas about how to fix code that isn't working?

Activity 1: TouchDevelop Creating a script using variables

TouchDevelop allows users to program apps for devices like smart phones and tablets. Variables are pieces of data that can change. In this activity you will write a script for an app that asks the user to enter their name and uses this to output a response.

1 Start by opening a new browser window and typing in **http://www.touchdevelop.com/app/** in the address bar. Then click on `Create Script` and then `blank` to open an empty script. Type in a name for your script, such as **Hello**. Then click on `create`. You will be asked your skill level: click on `coder`.

2 On the right of the screen is the edit area, where you write the code for the script. Click on `do nothing` in the edit area. This will bring up the code tools.

3 Click on the `var (new variable)` button at the bottom. This will allow you to define a new variable. In this program, the variable will be the user's name as this will change depending on who the user is. Then click after the red colon and equals symbol that appears next to it (:=).

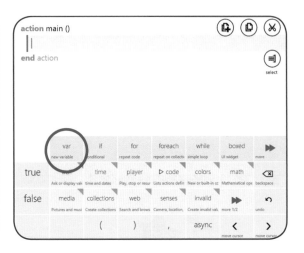

4

Click on the **wall** button. In TouchDevelop, the wall is where the code is displayed when the program is run. It is like the screen on a mobile device such as a smart phone or a tablet.

> This means that the variable will be displayed on the wall. In the next step, you will define what that variable is.

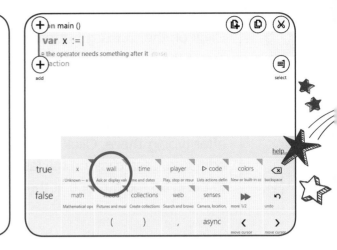

5

Click on the **ask string** button. A string is a fixed piece of text that can't be changed by the user. An ask string is a question that the user will need to respond to. You will notice that the *x* variable changes to *s*.

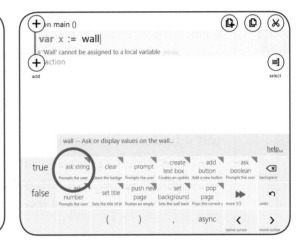

6

Make sure the cursor is after the speech marks, then click on the **edit** button. If the cursor isn't in the right place, the *edit* button won't be visible. Then type in **What is your name?**. The text you type in here will be the text the user sees when the script is run. Now click on the light blue area on the next line.

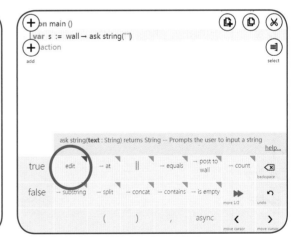

7

Click on the lower + button on the left. Then click on the **s** variable button, followed by the **assignment** button. The assignment button appears after you've clicked on the *s* variable button. Assignment operators allow the value of a variable (here it is *s*) to be updated.

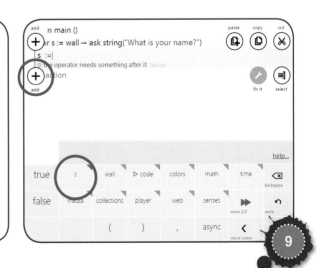

8

Click on the `string` button on the bottom left of the screen. It has "*abc*" on it and allows you to set the text that will be displayed on the wall of your app. Type in **Hey there** – make sure you add a space after typing **there**. Click anywhere in the edit area, then click on the last line of code to bring up the buttons at the bottom again.

9

Click on the `concat (concatenates two)` button. This will join two text strings together. Click inside the brackets and use the delete key or backspace button to remove the speech marks. Then click on the `s` button. This variable already stores whatever name the user entered when they were asked earlier. You are adding in a new string at the beginning of the current string.

10

Finally, click on the lower **+** button and then on the `s` button. Now click on the `post to wall` button. Click underneath the code you have just created.

```
action main ()
    var s := wall → ask string("What is your name?")
    s := "Hey there " → concat(s)
    s → post to wall
end action
```

11

It's now time to test your script, so click on the `run` button. Type in your name when asked and click OK. Watch as the computer replies using the name you entered.

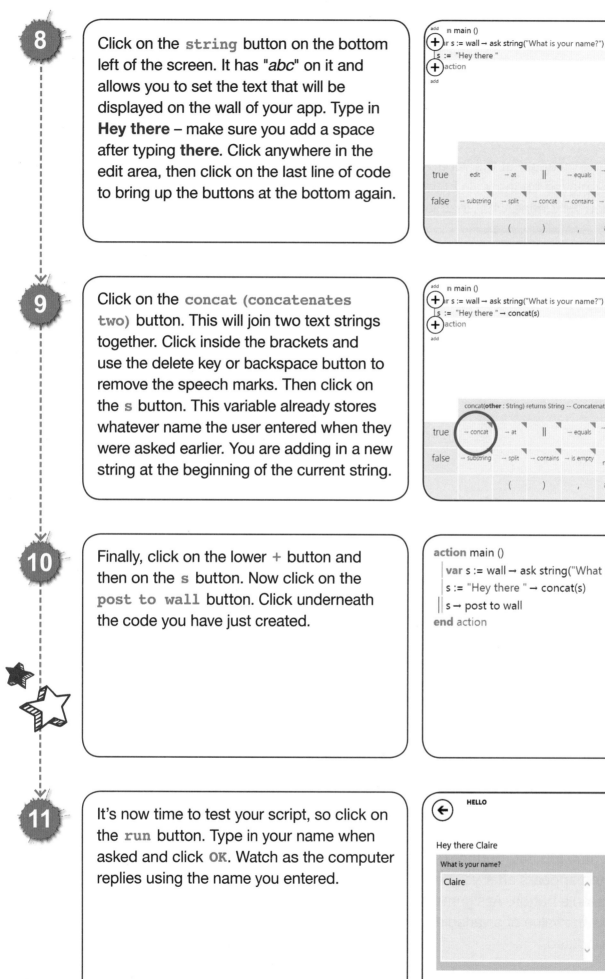

Now try this . . .

- Can you change the wording of the question to 'Can you tell me your name?'?

- Can you change the program's response from 'Hey there' to 'Hello' or 'Hi'?

- Can you add a second variable called *s2* and another ask string so the script asks the user their age and stores this in the *s2* variable?

- Can you add a response to concatenate a string with both the *s* and *s2* variables, such as 'Peter is 11'?

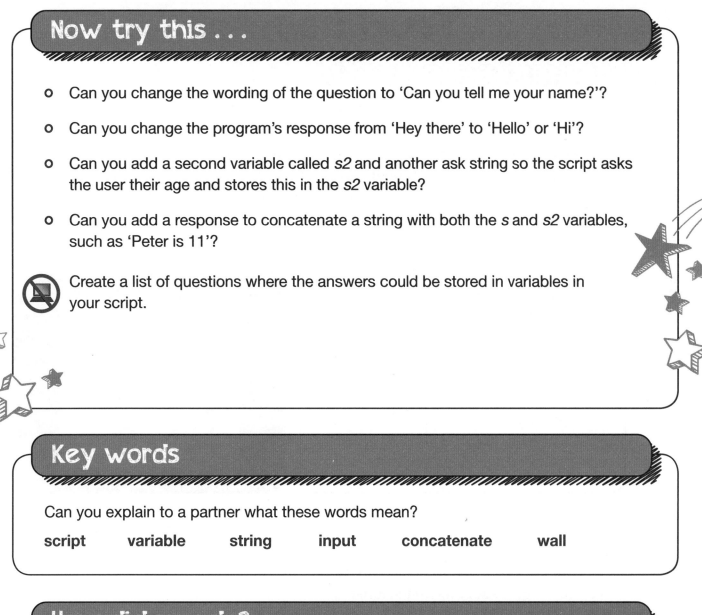 Create a list of questions where the answers could be stored in variables in your script.

Key words

Can you explain to a partner what these words mean?

script   **variable**   **string**   **input**   **concatenate**   **wall**

How did you do?

Think about what you did in this activity. Did you:

- create a script that uses variables to ask the user questions and respond to them?

- change the script to change the wording of the question?

- change the script to change the computer's response to the question?

- add a second variable to the script and use another ask string to ask the user a second question about their age and store their answer?

- add a response to the second question using the variable about the user's age?

Activity 2: TouchDevelop Programming a turtle

In the last activity, you built an app that used variables to ask the user for their name, store it and use it in a response. Now you are going to create an app that produces a different kind of output – drawings. You will also be exploring how using loops and repetition can make your code more efficient.

1 Type **http://www.touchdevelop.com/app/** in the address bar of a browser window and click on `Create Script`. Scroll down to select `blank turtle`. Type in a name for your script, such as **Drawing**. Then click on `create`. The turtle is used to produce drawings. As the turtle moves, its coloured pen leaves a trail behind it. This is very similar to how the program Logo works.

2 Click on `turtle ⟶ forward(100)` in the edit area to bring up the different commands. First we are going to program the turtle to move forward 200 steps. In the brackets, change *100* to **200**.

The turtle's four basic moves are forward, back, left turn and right turn.

3 What will happen when you run the program? Click on the `run` button on the left to see your code in action. The turtle should have moved forward as shown in the picture. If it didn't, go back and check your code to see what needs fixing. Click the `back arrow` button to take you back to editing the code.

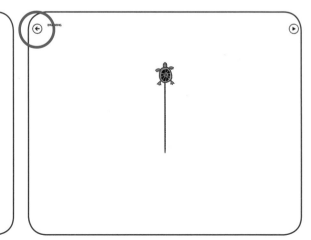

4 Click on the line of code and then click on the lower + button to add another line of code. Click on the **turtle** button and then click on **right turn**. If you can't see the button, click on the **more** button to see more buttons. The *90* between the brackets tells the turtle to turn 90 degrees to the right.

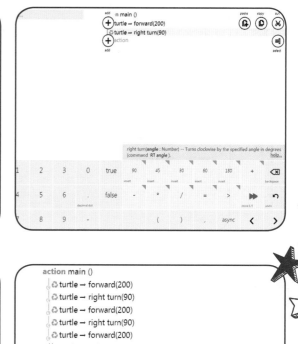

5 If you copied and pasted these two lines of code three more times, what shape do you think the turtle will draw? Use the **select** tool to select several lines of code by pulling the red handles up or down. Click **copy selection**. Place your cursor at the end of the last line of code and click **paste**. Run the program to see if your prediction was correct.

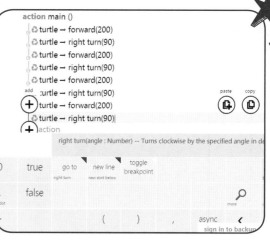

6 The turtle should have drawn a square. Do some debugging if this didn't happen. Instead of having to use these instructions four times, we could use loops that allow us to repeat code. Use the **select** tool to select all your code and delete it by clicking on the **delete selection** button that appears at the left of the screen.

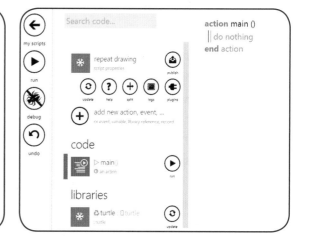

7 Click in the edit area, where it says *do nothing*, to bring up the commands. Click on **for**: this is the loop command. Each repetition in the loop is called an iteration. In the code, type in **4**. In your previous script you repeated the same two lines of code four times. Now the code nested inside the *for* command will be repeated four times.

8

Click underneath that line of code and then click on `turtle`, then `forward`. In the brackets, change *100* to **200**.

> Remember you need to type in how many steps it should move forward.

9

Click on the lower + button to add a line of code underneath. Start this line by clicking on `turtle` and then `right turn`.

10

Click on the white area underneath your program to have a look at the code. Read it through. What will happen when the turtle follows these commands?

> Remember the two lines of code nested underneath the *for* loop commands will be repeated four times.

11

Run your script to test it. Do you notice that it produces the same square that your first script did? This is what should happen. You have created two programs that produce the same output, but which one was easier to write and quicker to code? Why is that?

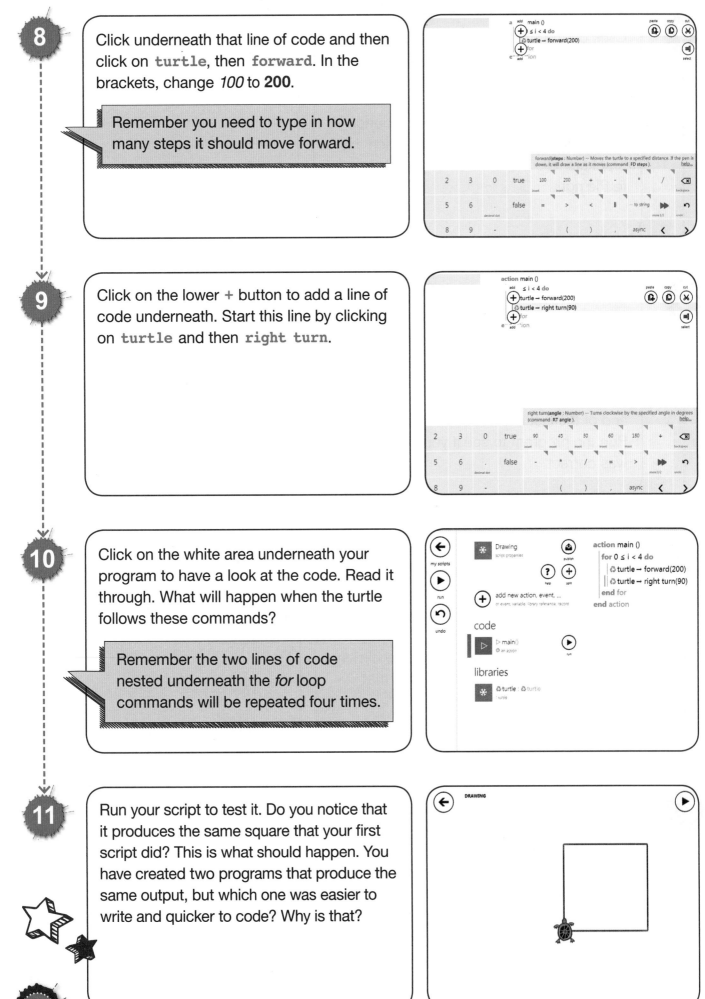

Now try this . . .

- Can you change the code so that it draws a larger square?

- Can you change the code to draw a smaller square?

- Can you add a line of code using the *set pen color* command to change the colour of the square the turtle draws?

- Can you program the turtle to draw other regular shapes such as an equilateral triangle or a regular hexagon?

Create your own turtle drawing code for a friend to follow. Can you come up with symbols to represent different drawing commands? Can you program your friend to draw different images communicating only using the symbols you have created?

Key words

Can you explain to a partner what these words mean?

turtle   **command**   **loop**   **repetition**   **output**

How did you do?

Think about what you did in this activity. Did you:

- create a script that uses loops to draw a square?

- change the script to draw a larger square?

- change the script to draw a smaller square?

- change the colour of the pen the turtle draws with?

- program the turtle to draw other regular shapes too?

Activity 3: TouchDevelop Drawing pixel by pixel

Images on screen are made up of a grid of pixels. In the last activity, you created an app that used a turtle to create drawings. Now you are going to explore using loops to create an image of a symmetrical snowflake, pixel by pixel.

1

Start by going to **https://www. touchdevelop.com/app/** in your web browser and clicking on `Create Script` as you did before. This time you are going to scroll down and click on the `blank pixel art` template. Give it a name, like **Pixel snowflake**.

2

Have a look at the code in the edit area. What do you think will happen when you run it? Run the script: you should see a 15 by 15 pixel grid with the pixel with coordinates (8,8) shaded.

The coordinates (8,8) tell the app where to paint. The colour has been set to random. If you run the script again, the pixel will be another colour.

3

Click on the `back arrow` to get back to the edit area. Now click on the second line of code and then click on the `select` button. Now it is highlighted green, the clipboard menu should appear. Click on `delete selection` to remove it.

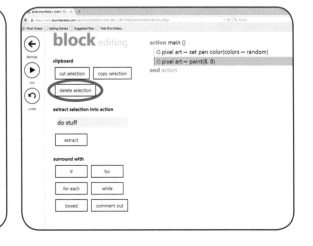

4

Click on the remaining line of code and then on the lower + sign to add a new line of code. You are going to add your first loop. Click on `for`. Where it asks you to insert a number, type **7**. This means that seven squares will be shaded. Then click on `do nothing` underneath to add another line of code.

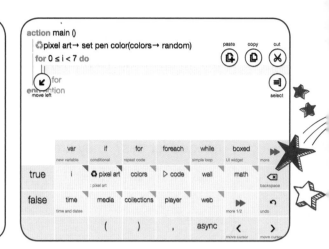

5

Now click on `pixel art`, then `paint`. Delete *0,0* and then use the on-screen keyboard to enter the coordinates **(8+i,8)**. Run the script. What do you expect to see? Remember to click the `back arrow` to get back to the edit area afterwards.

> This instructs the app to shade the pixel at (8,8) and then repeat this, adding one onto the *x* value each time, up to seven.

6

You should see a horizontal line of seven pixels shaded, going right from (8,8). Now let's draw a vertical line going downwards from (8,8). Click on the last line of code. Use the + button to add a new line. Click on `pixel art` and then `paint`. Delete *0,0* and enter the coordinates **(8,8+i)**. This will shade the pixel at (8,8) and repeat it, adding one onto the *y* value each time, up to seven.

```
action main ()
    pixel art→ set pen color(colors→ random)
    for 0 ≤ i < 7 do
        pixel art→ paint(8 + i, 8)
        pixel art→ paint(8, 8 + i)
    end for
end action
```

7

Let's create another horizontal line, starting at coordinate (8,8) but this time out to the left. Click on the last line of code and click the + button. Click on `pixel art`, then `paint`. Delete *0,0* and enter the coordinates **(8-i,8)**.

```
action main ()
    pixel art→ set pen color(colors→ random)
    for 0 ≤ i < 7 do
        pixel art→ paint(8 + i, 8)
        pixel art→ paint(8, 8 + i)
        pixel art→ paint(8 - i, 8)
    end for
end action
```

> We're using the minus sign this time because we're shading pixels in the opposite direction.

8

Now let's draw another vertical line. This one will go upwards from (8,8) so it's opposite the other vertical line. As before, start a new line of code and then click on `pixel art` and `paint`. Can you predict the coordinates needed for this? They are **(8,8-i)**.

```
action main ()
    ♻pixel art→ set pen color(colors→ random)
    for 0 ≤ i < 7 do
        ♻pixel art→ paint(8 + i, 8)
        ♻pixel art→ paint(8, 8 + i)
        ♻pixel art→ paint(8 - i, 8)
        ♻pixel art→ paint(8, 8 - i)
    end for
end action
```

9

What pattern will be created when you run the script? Try it. It should create a cross, like the one on the right. If not, you will need to debug your code and work out how to fix it.

10

To complete our snowflake, it needs four shorter diagonal lines coming from the centre. In the edit area, add a new line of code and a new loop by clicking the **for** button. Type in **3**, to make these lines short. Add another line of `pixel art` and `paint` code below, as you did before, with the coordinates **(8-j,8-j)**. This makes one line.

11

Now all that's needed to complete our snowflake is the other three short diagonal lines. Can you guess the coordinates needed in these lines of code? The first should be **(8+j,8-j)**, the second will be **(8+j,8+j)** and the third will be **(8-j,8+j)**. Run the script to see your finished snowflake.

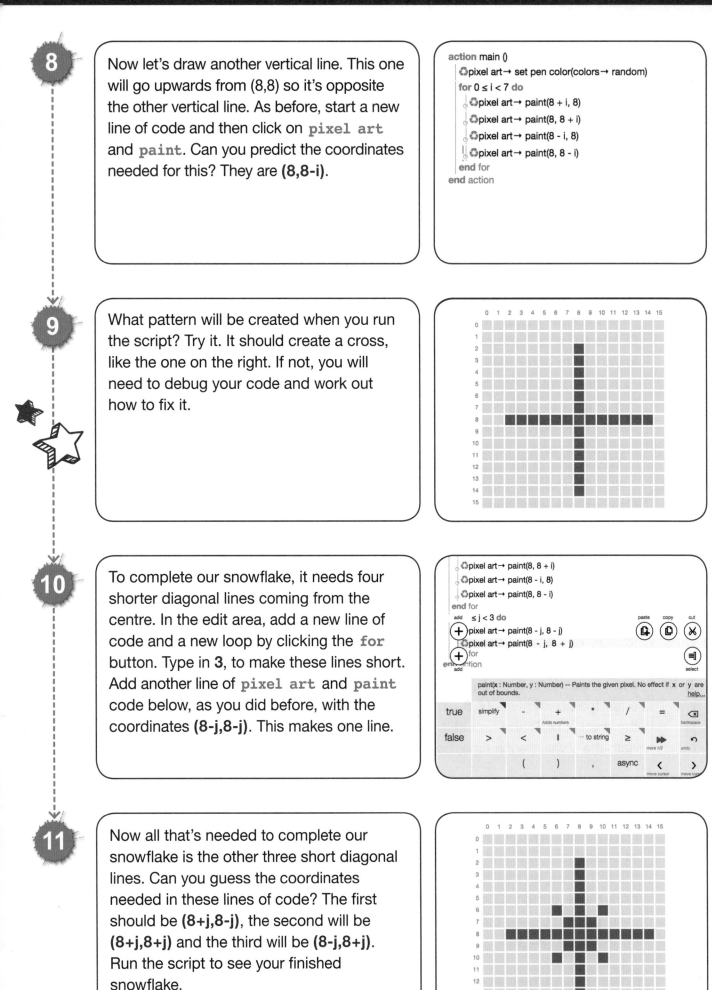

- Can you change the code so the pixels are shaded in a set colour each time, not just random colours?

- Can you make the four longer arms of your snowflake 5 pixels long instead of 7?

- Can you make the diagonal arms longer?

- Can you create other patterns with rotational symmetry?

- Use squared paper to create some pixel designs. Can you try to code some of your pixel designs?

Key words

Can you explain to a partner what these words mean?

pixel   **loop**   **repeat**   **command**

How did you do?

Think about what you did in this activity. Did you:

- create an app that draws a snowflake pixel by pixel?

- set your snowflake to be drawn in a specific colour?

- change the length of the arms of your snowflake?

- change the length of the diagonal arms?

- create apps that draw other patterns?

Activity 4: TouchDevelop Turning Scratch blocks into TouchDevelop scripts

Although TouchDevelop is a text-based coding language that uses text instead of blocks to create programs, you can mimic Scratch blocks in TouchDevelop, as you'll find in this activity.

1

Start by going to **http://www. touchdevelop.com/app/** in your web browser and then clicking on `Create Script`. This time you will select the `blank scratch` template. Type in a name like **Scratch animation**. This will load a blank template with the Scratch library for you to use.

2

Let's create a sprite first. You will use the variable *pic* to store a picture in the computer's memory. Click on `do nothing`, then click on `var`. Delete *x* and type in **pic**. Now click after the `:=` sign. In the *Search* box on the left, type **dog cartoon**. Click on an image to add it to the code.

3

Now the picture is stored as a variable, we can tell TouchDevelop that this image is a sprite. We will need another variable for this. Click on the lower + button, then click on `var` again. Delete *x* and type in **sprite**. Click after the `:=` sign and use the *Search* box to search for the `scratch new sprite` command. Click on it to add it to your code.

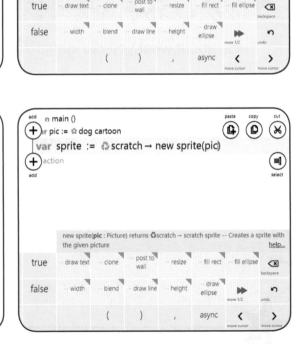

4

We want our animation to start when the user clicks the green flag so we need to add that command to our code. Click on the lower + button to add a new line of code. Use the *Search* box to look for the `when flag clicked` command. Click on it to add it to your code.

> When you use a Scratch command, it is then saved under the *scratch* button ready to use again.

```
action main ()
    var pic := ✿ dog cartoon
    var sprite := ♻ scratch → new sprite(pic)
    ♻ scratch → when flag clicked(clicked)
        where clicked() is
            do nothing
    end
end action
```

5

To program the dog to say 'Woof!' in a speech bubble for two seconds when the green flag is clicked, click on `do nothing` below the *where clicked () is* code. Click on `sprite`. Search for the `say for` command and click on it to add it to your code. Use the backspace to delete the *0* and type in **2**. Click on the speech marks and click on `edit`. Type in **Woof!**.

```
action main ()
    var pic := ✿ dog cartoon
    var sprite := ♻ scratch → new sprite(pic)
    ♻ scratch → when flag clicked(clicked)
        where clicked() is
            sprite → say for("Woof!", 2)
    end
end action
```

6

Now you are going to use repetition to move the sprite back and forth. Click on the last line of code and then the + button to add a new line. Click on `for` and then enter the number **10** into the code.

> The *for ... do* loop is similar to the repeat command in Scratch. Any code after this will be repeated 10 times.

```
action main ()
    var pic := ✿ dog cartoon
    var sprite := ♻ scratch → new sprite(pic)
    ♻ scratch → when flag clicked(clicked)
        where clicked() is
            sprite → say for("Woof!", 2)
            for 0 ≤ i < 10 do
                do nothing
            end for
    end
    do nothing
end action
```

7

Click underneath the *for* line of code where it says `do nothing` and then click on `sprite`. Search for the `scratch move(steps)` command and click on it to add it to your script. Where it says *0*, change it to **30**. This instructs the sprite to move 30 steps to the right. A negative number would program it to move to the left.

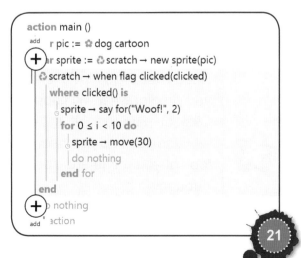

```
action main ()
add     r pic := ✿ dog cartoon
(+)    r sprite := ♻ scratch → new sprite(pic)
        ♻ scratch → when flag clicked(clicked)
            where clicked() is
                sprite → say for("Woof!", 2)
                for 0 ≤ i < 10 do
                    sprite → move(30)
                    do nothing
                end for
    end
(+) o nothing
add   action
```

8

Click on the line underneath again and use the + button to add a new line. Use the *Search* box to find the `scratch wait(seconds)` command. Click on it to add it to your code. Where it says *0*, change it to **1**.

> This will instruct the sprite to wait for 1 second before following the next command.

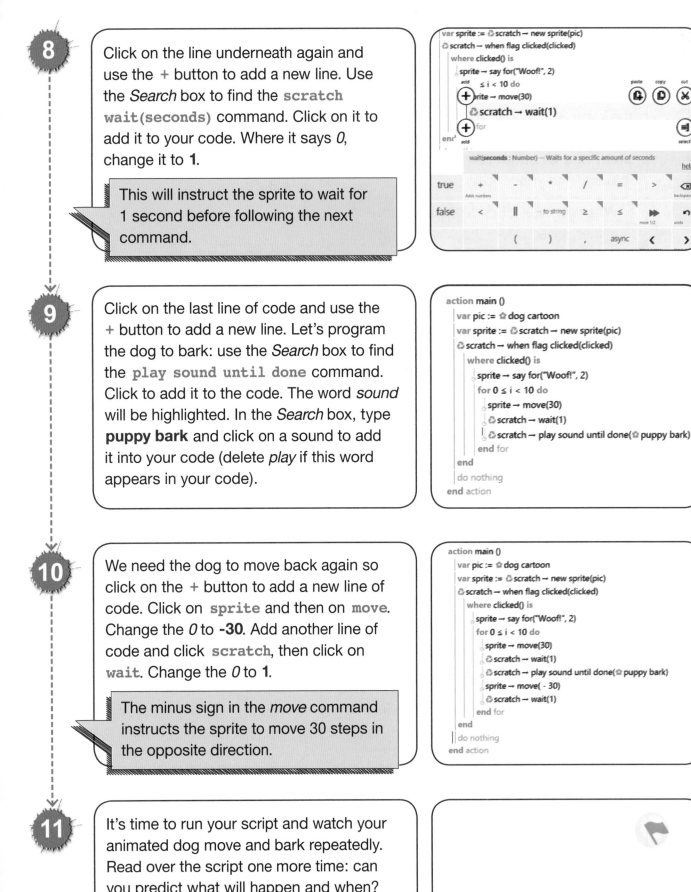

```
var sprite := ☼ scratch → new sprite(pic)
☼ scratch → when flag clicked(clicked)
  where clicked() is
    sprite → say for("Woof!", 2)
    ≤ i < 10 do
  ⊕ rite → move(30)
      ☼ scratch → wait(1)
  ⊕ for
end
```

wait(**seconds** : Number) — Waits for a specific amount of seconds   help...

true   +   -   *   /   =   >   ⌫
        Adds numbers   backspace

false   <   ‖   to string   ≥   ≤   ►►   ↺
                                         more 1/2   undo

        (   )   ,   async   <   >

9

Click on the last line of code and use the + button to add a new line. Let's program the dog to bark: use the *Search* box to find the `play sound until done` command. Click to add it to the code. The word *sound* will be highlighted. In the *Search* box, type **puppy bark** and click on a sound to add it into your code (delete *play* if this word appears in your code).

```
action main ()
  var pic := ☼ dog cartoon
  var sprite := ☼ scratch → new sprite(pic)
  ☼ scratch → when flag clicked(clicked)
    where clicked() is
      sprite → say for("Woof!", 2)
      for 0 ≤ i < 10 do
        sprite → move(30)
        ☼ scratch → wait(1)
        ☼ scratch → play sound until done(☼ puppy bark)
      end for
  end
  do nothing
end action
```

10

We need the dog to move back again so click on the + button to add a new line of code. Click on `sprite` and then on `move`. Change the *0* to **-30**. Add another line of code and click `scratch`, then click on `wait`. Change the *0* to **1**.

> The minus sign in the *move* command instructs the sprite to move 30 steps in the opposite direction.

```
action main ()
  var pic := ☼ dog cartoon
  var sprite := ☼ scratch → new sprite(pic)
  ☼ scratch → when flag clicked(clicked)
    where clicked() is
      sprite → say for("Woof!", 2)
      for 0 ≤ i < 10 do
        sprite → move(30)
        ☼ scratch → wait(1)
        ☼ scratch → play sound until done(☼ puppy bark)
        sprite → move( - 30)
        ☼ scratch → wait(1)
      end for
  end
  do nothing
end action
```

11

It's time to run your script and watch your animated dog move and bark repeatedly. Read over the script one more time: can you predict what will happen and when? Click on `run` to try it. If it doesn't quite work as you had planned, you will need to look at your code and spend some time debugging it.

Now try this . . .

- Can you change the number of times the dog moves back and forth?

- Can you change what the dog says at the beginning?

- Can you change the number of steps he moves?

- Can you change the input by searching for and using the *sprite when clicked(clicked2)* command so the animation begins when the sprite is clicked instead of the flag?

- Create a storyboard for a character that you could animate in this way.

Key words

Can you explain to a partner what these words mean?

command   **repeat**   **variable**   **input**   **sequence**   **sprite**   **for ... do loop**

How did you do?

Think about what you did in this activity. Did you:

- animate a sprite by coding Scratch blocks in TouchDevelop?

- change the number of times the sprite moves repeatedly?

- change what the sprite says?

- change the number of steps the sprite moves?

- change how the animation is started?

Activity 5: App Inventor Programming a button

For this activity, an adult will need to help you find a copyright-free image and sound effect of a dice online.

App Inventor allows you to design and program your own apps. You are going to build a virtual dice app and then adapt it for different purposes. First you will program a button to make a sound when it is clicked.

1

Start by typing **http://ai2.appinventor. mit.edu/** into your web browser. Click on `Projects` and then `Start new project` in the drop-down menu. Type in a name, such as **dice_app**, and click `OK`.

> You will need a Google Apps for Education account to use App Inventor. Ask an adult to help you with this.

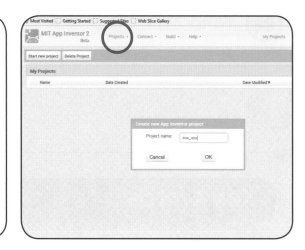

2

On the left side of the screen are palettes containing different components you might want to use in your app. In the *User Interface* palette, click on the `Button` component and drag it into the *Viewer* in the middle of the screen.

> The *Viewer* shows what your app will look like on a mobile device such as a tablet.

3

Now we will put an image of a dice on the button. First click on the button component in the *Viewer*. In the *Properties* pane, click in the box under the word *Image* and then on `Upload File…`. Click on `Choose File` and locate the dice image file saved on your computer. Click `OK`. You should see the dice image in the *Viewer* now.

4

In the *Properties* pane, go to the *Text* field and delete the *Text for Button 1* text. Click in the *Viewer* to update it. You should now see only the dice image in the *Viewer*, without the text.

5

Next you will program the button to make a sound when clicked. Go to the *Palette* pane on the left and click on `Media` in the menu (towards the bottom of your screen). Drag a `Sound` component into the *Viewer*.

A *Sound* component cannot be seen in the *Viewer*. You can see it at the bottom in the *Non-visible components* section.

6

Click on the `Sound` component so you can see its properties in the *Properties* pane on the right. Click in the box underneath where it says *Source* and then on `Upload File`.... Click on `Choose File` and find the audio file of the dice being rolled. Click `Open` and then `OK` to upload it. You should now see the audio file name underneath where it says *Source*.

7

Now the button and sound components are in place, it's time to use the *Blocks* editor to program them. Remember, you are going to program the button to play the dice roll sound when it is clicked. Click on `Blocks` in the top right-hand corner of your screen to edit the blocks.

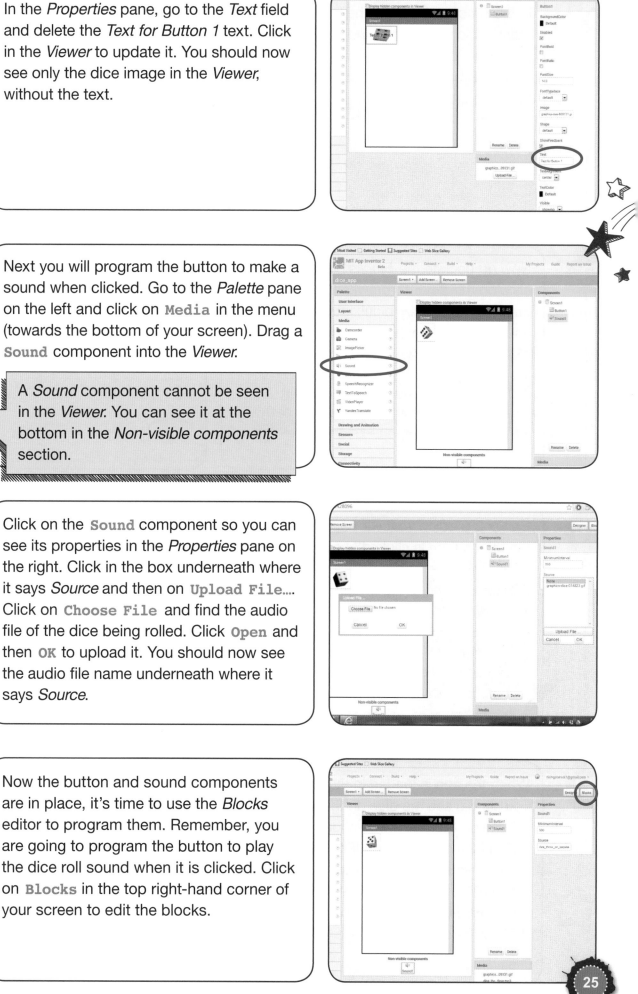

25

8

In the *Blocks* palette on the left, there are menus such as *Control* and *Logic*. These are called 'drawers'. Click on the `Button1` drawer. Drag a `when Button1 Click ... do` block into the *Viewer*.

9

Now go back to the *Blocks* palette and click on the `Sound1` drawer. Drag a `call Sound1 Play` block into the *Viewer* and snap it inside the `when Button1 Click ... do` block.

> You'll hear a snap sound when the blocks have been connected properly.

10

Can you predict what will happen when the dice button is clicked? Let's test how it will look on a mobile device. Click on `Connect` at the top and then `Emulator` in the drop-down menu.

> The emulator simulates the screen of a mobile device so you can test your app in action. An adult will need to install the aiStarter on your computer.

11

When the app is loaded in the emulator, you should see the dice on the screen. When you click on it, you should hear the rolling dice sound effect. If it is not working quite as you want it to, go back and do some debugging. Click on `Projects` and `Save project` as you will be using this in the next three activities.

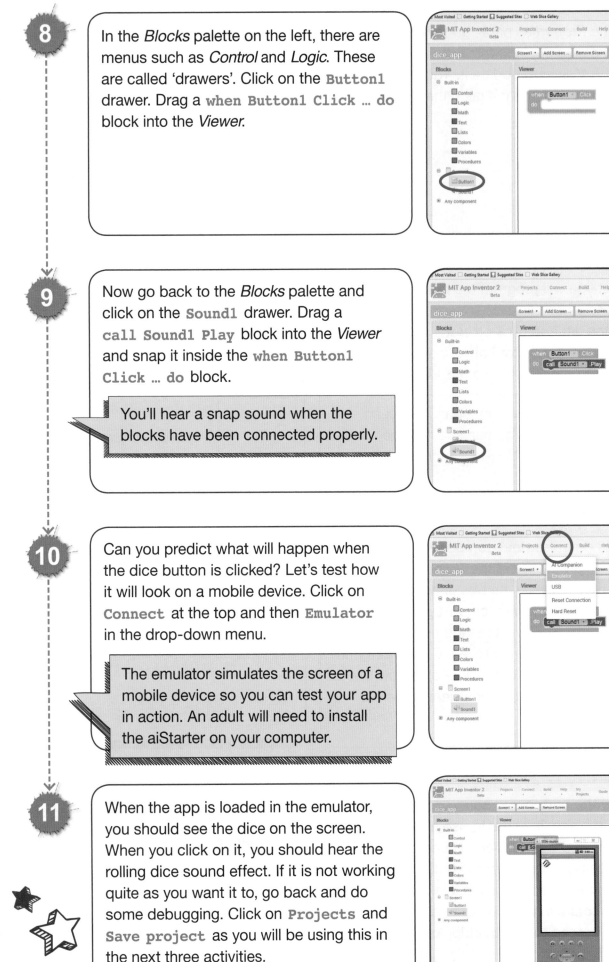

Now try this . . .

- Can you change the image for the button?

- Can you try using other sound effects?

- Can you create your own image?

- Can you use the *call Sound1 vibrate* block so the device vibrates when the button is clicked as well as playing the sound effect?

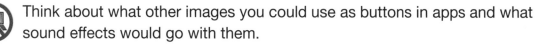 Think about what other images you could use as buttons in apps and what sound effects would go with them.

Key words

Can you explain to a partner what these words mean?

app   **block**   **command**   **debug**   **emulator**   **upload**

How did you do?

Think about what you did in this activity. Did you:

- create an app that has a button that makes a sound when clicked?

- change the button image?

- try different sound effects?

- create and use your own images?

- program the emulator so it vibrates when the button is clicked?

Activity 6: App Inventor Picking random numbers

The next step is to program the dice button to pick a random number between 1 and 6 when clicked using the *random integer* block.

1 Start by going to **http://ai2.appinventor. mit.edu** in your web browser. Click on `Projects` and then `My projects` to bring up all your saved projects. Click on the `dice_app` project you saved last time to load it.

2 First we are going to think about the user interface – where the different components are on the screen. Go to the *Palette* pane and click on `Layout`. Drag the `VerticalArrangement` component into the *Viewer*. It looks like an empty box at this point, but it will line up vertically any components that you put in it.

3 Go back to the *Palette* and click on `User Interface`. Drag a `Label` component into the *VerticalArrangement* box in the *Viewer*. This label is going to instruct the user how to use the app.

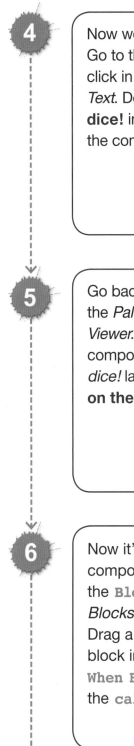

4

Now we are going to change the *Label* text. Go to the *Properties* pane on the right and click in the box underneath where it says *Text*. Delete the text and type in **Roll the dice!** instead. Click in the *Viewer* to update the component in the *Viewer*.

5

Go back to the *User Interface* section of the *Palette* and drag another label into the *Viewer*. Drag it into the *VerticalArrangement* component so it sits underneath the *Roll the dice!* label. Change the text so it reads **Click on the dice to find out your number....**

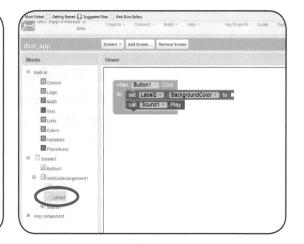

6

Now it's time to program these new components in the *Blocks* editor. Click on the `Blocks` button on the top right. In the *Blocks* palette, click on the `Label2` drawer. Drag a `set Label2 BackgroundColor to` block into the *Viewer*. Snap it in the `When Button1 click ... do` block, above the `call Sound1 Play` block.

7

You are now going to change the *Label2* block because you need to program its text, not its colour. You want the label to display a random number from 1 to 6 when the button is clicked. Click on the second drop-down menu in the green block and change it from *BackgroundColor* to `Text`.

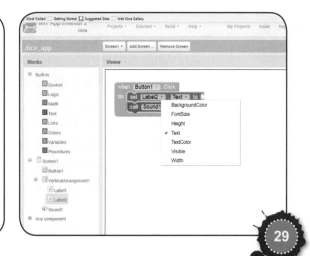

29

8

In the *Blocks* palette, click on the `Math` drawer. Drag a `random integer from` block into the *Viewer* and connect it with the `set Label2 Text to` block. Remember: an integer is a whole number.

> This will set the text in *Label2* to a random number between 1 and 100 when the button is clicked.

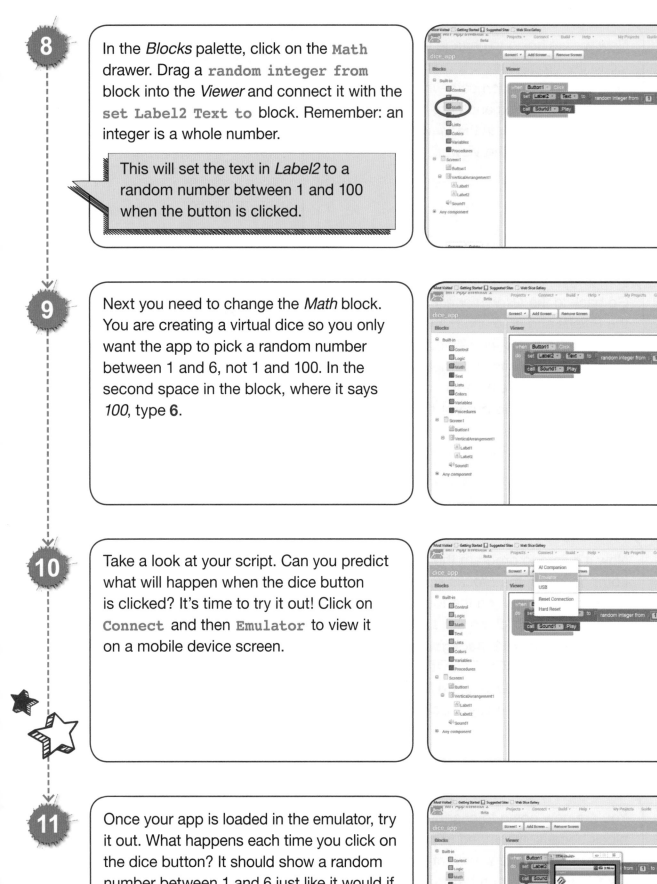

9

Next you need to change the *Math* block. You are creating a virtual dice so you only want the app to pick a random number between 1 and 6, not 1 and 100. In the second space in the block, where it says *100*, type **6**.

10

Take a look at your script. Can you predict what will happen when the dice button is clicked? It's time to try it out! Click on `Connect` and then `Emulator` to view it on a mobile device screen.

11

Once your app is loaded in the emulator, try it out. What happens each time you click on the dice button? It should show a random number between 1 and 6 just like it would if you rolled an actual dice. If it isn't working, go back and look over your code again. It may need some debugging. Save your project ready for the next activity.

Now try this . . .

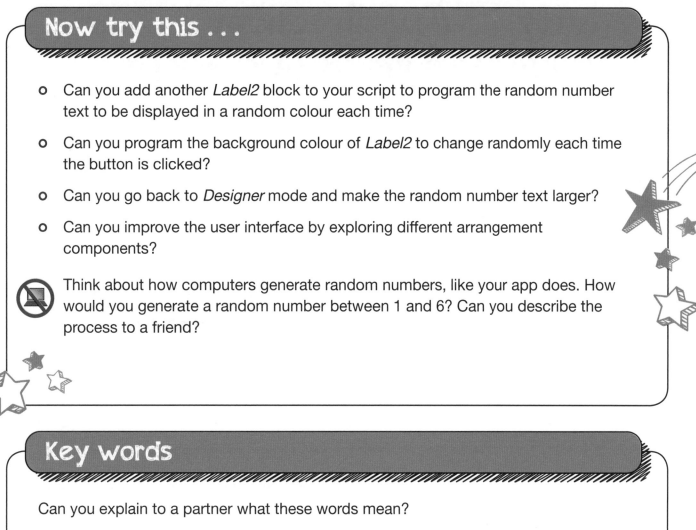

- Can you add another *Label2* block to your script to program the random number text to be displayed in a random colour each time?

- Can you program the background colour of *Label2* to change randomly each time the button is clicked?

- Can you go back to *Designer* mode and make the random number text larger?

- Can you improve the user interface by exploring different arrangement components?

Think about how computers generate random numbers, like your app does. How would you generate a random number between 1 and 6? Can you describe the process to a friend?

Key words

Can you explain to a partner what these words mean?

program   **random**   **select**   **interface**   **button**   **label**

How did you do?

Think about what you did in this activity. Did you:

- program the emulator to play a sound and display a random number when it is clicked?

- change the script to change the colour of the random number text?

- change the script so the background colour of the random number also changes when the button is clicked?

- change the size of the text of the random number?

- improve the user interface by changing the layout of the components?

Activity 7: App Inventor Changing the input and output

We can now explore other forms of input and output. You will program the dice app to work when the mobile device is shaken (this won't work on the emulator) and have the result spoken, as well as displayed on screen.

1 Start by typing **http://ai2.appinventor.mit.edu** into your web browser. Then click on **Projects** and **My projects**. Click on the **dice_app** project you saved last time to load it.

2 In the *Palette* pane, click on the **Sensors** section. Drag an **AccelerometerSensor** component into the *Viewer*. This allows the mobile device to detect movement. You are going to use this so the virtual dice is rolled when the mobile device is shaken.

> This component can't be seen so it sits in the *Non-visible components* section.

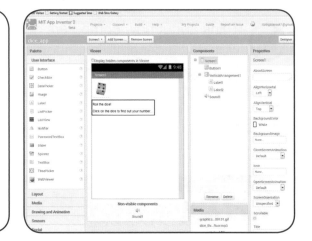

3 Now click on **Blocks** to change how the app is programmed. At the moment the dice is rolled when the dice button is clicked; you are going to change this. In the *Blocks* palette, click on the **AccelerometerSensor1** drawer.

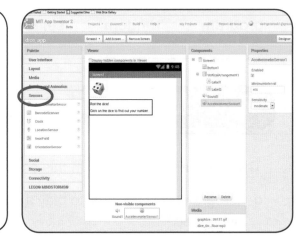

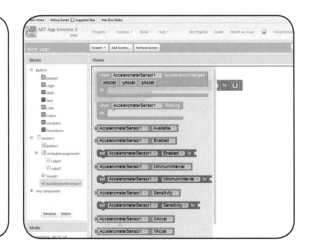

4

Next drag a `When AccelerometerSensor1 shaking… do` block into the *Viewer*. Right-click on the `set Label2 text to…` block and select `Duplicate`. Drag the copied block into the `When AccelerometerSensor1 shaking… do` block. Now do the same with the `call Sound1 Play` block.

5

The dice app should now display a random number between 1 and 6 when the device is shaken. To test this, you will need an Android mobile device as shaking cannot be simulated on the emulator. Click on `Connect` and `AI Companion` to display a QR code. Scan this using the *AI2 Companion* app on a device that runs the Android operating system to test the app.

6

Now let's focus on outputting the number thrown by our virtual dice as speech as well as displaying the number. Click on `Designer` (top right of screen) as we need to add a new component to do this. In the *Palette* pane, click on `Media`. Drag a `TextToSpeech` component into the *Viewer*.

It's a non-visible component so it appears at the bottom of the screen.

7

We now need to program the *TextToSpeech* component so click on `Blocks` to use the *Blocks* editor. In the *Blocks* palette, click on the `TextToSpeech1` drawer to see this component's blocks.

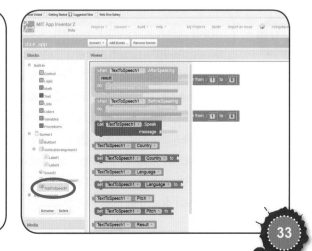

8

Drag a `call TextToSpeech1 Speak message` block into the *Viewer*. Insert it into the `When Button1 Click ... do` block, underneath the other blocks. This means when the dice button is clicked, the *TextToSpeech* component will be used, but we still need to tell it what text we want it to say.

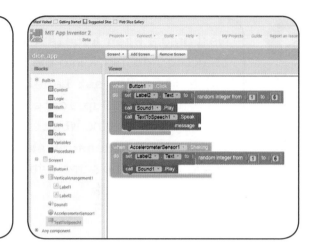

9

Click on the `Label2` drawer and drag a `Label2 Text` block into the *Viewer*. Snap it onto the `call TextToSpeech1 Speak message` block. This tells the *TextToSpeech* component to say whatever the *Label2* text is. Remember the *Label2* text is a random number between 1 and 6. The app should now say the number out loud and display it in *Label2*.

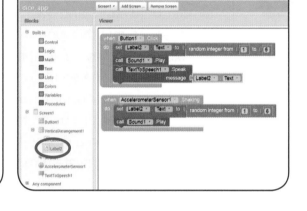

10

Right-click on the `call TextToSpeech1 Speak message` block and select `Duplicate`. Insert the duplicated blocks into the `When AccelerometerSensor1 shaking... do` block. This makes the *TextToSpeak* component work whether the input is the button being clicked or the mobile device being shaken.

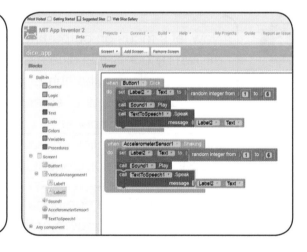

11

Take a look at your script. Can you predict what will happen when the button is clicked? Test it using the emulator. Click on `Connect` and then `Emulator`. Alternatively, test it on an Android device if you have one. When you click the dice, a random number between 1 and 6 should be displayed by the app and read out loud. Save your project for the next activity.

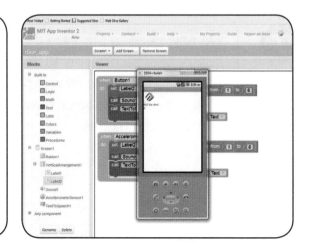

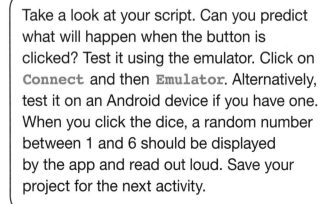

Now try this . . .

- Can you make the dice button rotate when it is clicked or the device is shaken?

- Can you use another *TextToSpeech* component to program the app to speak the instruction 'Roll the dice'?

- Can you program the app to play different sounds depending on what number is rolled?

- Can you get the app to roll two dice and add the results together?

Think about how a computer turns text to speech. Are there any sounds that might be tricky for a computer to produce? What combinations of letters produce different sounds? How will a computer know what sound to use?

Key words

Can you explain to a partner what these words mean?

program   **input**   **output**   **random**   **text-to-speech**   **accelerometer**

How did you do?

Think about what you did in this activity. Did you:

- create an app that uses clicking and shaking as input, and text and sound as output?

- change the script to make the dice button rotate when it is clicked or the device is shaken?

- use another *TextToSpeech* component to program the app to speak the instructions and to display them on the screen?

- program the app to play different sounds depending on the number rolled?

- get the app to add together the results of two dice rolls?

Activity 8: App Inventor Adapting an app

You have created an app that simulates rolling a dice by selecting random data. Here you will adapt the dice app to create an app that produces random story settings using lists. Lists allow a program to store information: we will program it to pick items from that list randomly.

1 Start by typing **http://ai2.appinventor. mit.edu** into your web browser. Click on **Projects** and then **My projects**. Double-click on **dice_app** to open it. Then click on **Projects** again but this time go to **Save project as …** and give it another name like **settings_app**.

> We will adapt our script not start a new one.

2 Let's start by changing the button to match the purpose of the new app. Click on the dice button in the *Viewer*. In the *Properties* pane, click in the box under the *Image* section. In the menu that pops up, select **None** and click **OK**. This removes the dice image. Click in the box under *Text* and type in **Magic!**.

3 Click on **Label1** and change the *Text* from *Roll the dice!* to **Find a story setting!**. Click on **Label2** and change the *Text* to **Click on the magic button to get a super story setting....**

4

You need to remove the rolling dice sound effect as this no longer fits in with the purpose of your new app. Click on `Sound1` in the *Components* list on the right and then click on the `Delete` button below. Then click `OK`.

The sound will disappear from the *Non-visible components* section too.

5

You need to change how *Button1* and *Label2* are programmed because they are going to produce a story setting rather than a random number. Click on `Blocks`. Delete the `random integer from` block by dragging it off and dropping it over the bin. Click `OK`. Delete all the blocks in the middle of the `When AccelerometerSensor1 shaking…` `do` block in the same way. Click `OK`.

6

In the *Blocks* palette, click on the `Lists` drawer. Drag a `pick a random item list` block into the *Viewer* and snap onto the `set Label2 Text to` block. From the `Lists` drawer, click on a `make a list` block and snap it next to the `pick a random item list` block.

The app will randomly pick from story settings you add to this list.

7

Go to the `Text` drawer and drag out a `" … "` block. Snap this onto the `make a list` block. Type a story setting into the block. Repeat this, but type in a different story setting.

You need more than two settings for your app to pick from to make it interesting, but it looks like the *make a list* block is full, doesn't it?

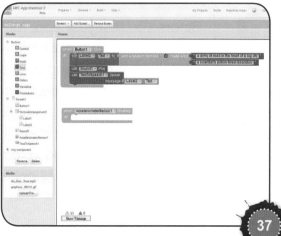

37

8

To add more story settings, click on the dark blue button on the `make a list` block. Drag `item` blocks into the *list* block in the pop-up window. The number of blocks you put in will be how many story settings you can add to your list. Add at least three more.

> The *make a list* block is known as a mutator block because you can change its size.

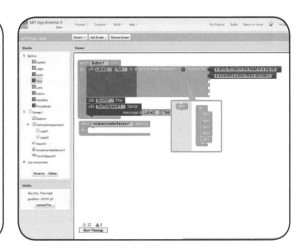

9

Use " ... " blocks to add three more settings to your `make a list` block.

> Remember these are the settings your app will randomly choose for the user each time they click the *Magic!* button or shake the device the app is running on.

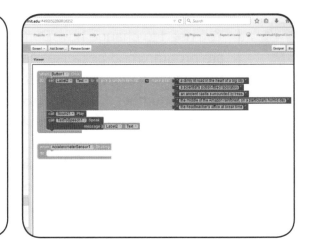

10

When the story settings are done, right-click on all the blocks nested in the `when Button1 Click ... do` block and duplicate them. Then insert them all in the `When AccelerometerSensor1 shaking... do` block.

> This means the app will work whether the *Magic!* button is clicked or the device is shaken.

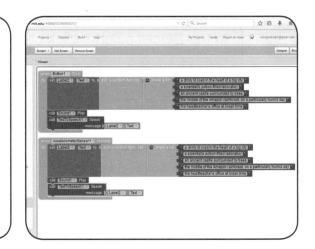

11

Before you test your app, run through the code. Can you predict what will happen? Click on `Connect` and then `Emulator`. Click on the `Magic!` button several times. Different settings from your list should be displayed randomly and spoken out loud. If something isn't working, go back to the code and do some debugging to fix it.

Now try this . . .

- Can you add more story settings? Perhaps a list of 10 for the app to choose from?

- Can you combine multiple random picks from different lists into the same label text?

- Can you create an app that randomly picks pupils from your class? How could this be used? Can you ensure picked names are removed so the same person doesn't get picked twice?

- Can you change your code and use a procedure or function to avoid duplicating so many blocks?

Brainstorm other apps that you could make by adapting this one. Remember that it is based on selecting items from a list at random.

Key words

Can you explain to a partner what these words mean?

program   **simulate**   **selection**   **input**   **output**   **debug**   **list**

How did you do?

Think about what you did in this activity. Did you:

- adapt your dice app to create a story settings app?

- change the script to add more settings?

- combine multiple random picks from different lists into the same label text?

- create a random name picker app based on this one?

- use a procedure or function to take out some of the duplication in your code?

Activity 9: Python The print command

Python is a text-based programming language and IDLE is a Python interpreter. It reads the programs written in Python and executes the instructions one at a time. The steps below explore how to create a program that instructs your computer to display messages and use the repetition command to repeat messages.

1

Python 3.4.2 can be downloaded at **www.python.org/downloads**. Start IDLE from your *Programs* menu. Click on the `File` menu and then on `New File` to open the *Code* window. There are two different windows: the *Shell* window and the *Code* window. The *Code* window is where you write the code and the *Shell* window is where the output appears when you run the program.

```
File  Edit  Shell  Debug  Options  Windows  Help
                              :023a9432, Oct  6 2014, 22:
New File        Ctrl+N
Open...         Ctrl+O         s" or "license()" for more
Recent Files               ▶
Open Module...  Alt+M
Class Browser   Alt+C
Path Browser

Save            Ctrl+S
Save As...      Ctrl+Shift+S
Save Copy As... Alt+Shift+S

Print Window    Ctrl+P

Close           Alt+F4
Exit            Ctrl+Q
```

2

Now you can enter some code in the *Code* window. Type in **print('Hello, World!')**. The words between the single speech marks will be the message the computer displays when the program is run. A 'Hello, World!' is traditionally the first program that people use when learning a new programming language.

```
*Untitled*
File  Edit  Format  Run  Options  Windows  Help
print('Hello, World!')
```

3

Click on `File` and then `Save` to save your Python code file, which will end with the extension *.py*.

You must save code before Python will run a program. If you forget and try to run a program that hasn't been saved, IDLE will alert you with a warning message.

```
*Untitled*
File  Edit  Format  Run  Options  Windows  Help

New File        Ctrl+N
Open...         Ctrl+O
Recent Files               ▶
Open Module...  Alt+M
Class Browser   Alt+C
Path Browser

Save            Ctrl+S
Save As...      Ctrl+Shift+S
Save Copy As... Alt+Shift+S

Print Window    Ctrl+P

Close           Alt+F4
Exit            Ctrl+Q
```

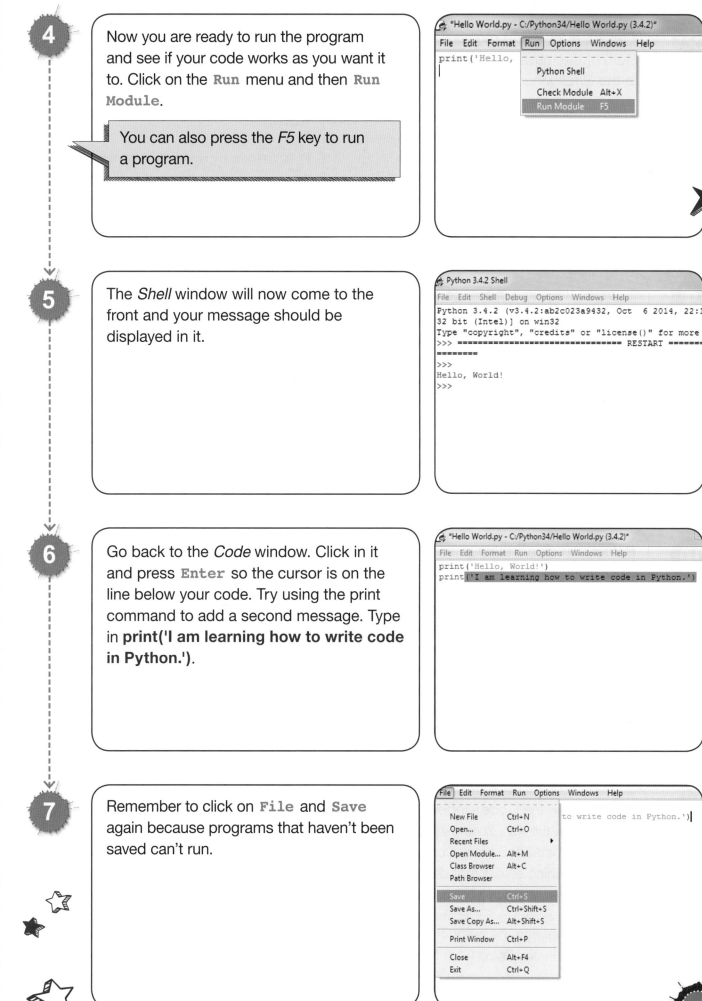

4 Now you are ready to run the program and see if your code works as you want it to. Click on the **Run** menu and then **Run Module**.

You can also press the *F5* key to run a program.

5 The *Shell* window will now come to the front and your message should be displayed in it.

6 Go back to the *Code* window. Click in it and press **Enter** so the cursor is on the line below your code. Try using the print command to add a second message. Type in **print('I am learning how to write code in Python.')**.

7 Remember to click on **File** and **Save** again because programs that haven't been saved can't run.

8

Press the **F5** key to run your updated code. Both of the messages should now appear in the *Shell* window.

File Edit Shell Debug Options Windows Help

```
File  Edit  Shell  Debug  Options  Windows  Help
Python 3.4.2 (v3.4.2:ab2c023a9432, Oct  6 2014, 22
32 bit (Intel)] on win32
Type "copyright", "credits" or "license()" for mor
>>> ============================= RESTART =====
========
>>>
Hello, World!
>>> ============================= RESTART =====
========
>>>
Hello, World!
I am learning how to write code in Python.
>>>
```

9

To make the same message repeat, on a new line type in **for i in range (5):**. Press **Enter**. Type in **print('Save your code before you run it.')**. This line of code has been indented: this affects its meaning. It shows that this line of code is the one that should follow the repetition command above it. This will repeat the message five times.

```
File  Edit  Format  Run  Options  Windows  Help
print('Hello, World!')
print('I am learning how to write code in Python.')
for i in range (5):
    print('Save your code before you run it.')
```

10

Before you do anything else, save the code. Now press **F5** to run the program. The last message will be displayed five times.

```
File  Edit  Shell  Debug  Options  Windows  Help
Python 3.4.2 (v3.4.2:ab2c023a9432, Oct  6 2014, 22:15:05) [MSC v
32 bit (Intel)] on win32
Type "copyright", "credits" or "license()" for more information.
>>> ============================= RESTART ================
========
>>>
Hello, World!
>>> ============================= RESTART ================
========
>>>
Hello, World!
I am learning how to write code in Python.
>>> ============================= RESTART ================
========
>>>
Hello, World!
I am learning how to write code in Python.
Save your code before you run it.
Save your code before you run it.
Save your code before you run it.
Save your code before you run it.
Save your code before you run it.
>>>
```

11

Click back in the *Code* window. Delete the number *5* in the *for i in range (5):* code and type in **10** instead. Save the code before you do anything else. What do you think will happen when you run it? Press **F5** to try it.

> This will change the number of times the message is displayed from five to 10.

```
File  Edit  Format  Run  Options  Windows  Help
print('Hello, World!')
print('I am learning how to write code in Python.')
for i in range (10):
    print('Save your code before you run it.')
```

42

Now try this . . .

- ○ Can you use the print command to display a message that says what your name is?

- ○ Can you write a program that repeats a message three times?

- ○ Can you create a program that displays a different set of three messages?

- ○ Can you add in code so those three messages are repeated twice?

 Write out a simple Python program and ask your friend to take on the role of the Python interpreter. Can they follow your code correctly and produce the messages that you intended?

Key words

Can you explain to a partner what these words mean?

command **print** **code** **run** **program** **interpreter**

How did you do?

Think about what you did in this activity. Did you:

- ○ create a program that displays a message?

- ○ change the code to display a message that says what your name is?

- ○ add in the code so the message about your name is repeated three times?

- ○ create a program that displays a different set of three messages?

- ○ add in the correct code so your different messages are repeated?

Activity 10: Python The input function

In the last activity, you used the print and repetition commands to create a program that displayed messages to the user. Now you are going to explore the input command and variables to create a program that asks the user questions and then uses that information.

1 Start IDLE and open the *Code* window by clicking on `File` and then `New File`. Click in the *Code* window and type in **print('Hello and welcome.')**.

```
*Untitled*
File  Edit  Format  Run  Options  Windows  Help
print('Hello and welcome.')
```

2 Press `Enter` so you are on a new line. Type in **name=input('What is your name?')**. When the program is run, this will ask the user for their name and wait for them to type it in. It will store this as the *name* variable so it can be used later. Remember that a variable is a piece of data that can be changed.

```
*Untitled*
File  Edit  Format  Run  Options  Windows  Help
print('Hello and welcome.')
name=input('What is your name?')
```

3 Press `Enter` again. Type in **print('It is great to meet you', name)**. Click on `File` and then `Save`. Press `F5` and run the code. When the program is run, it will put whatever name the user entered where the word 'name' is.

```
Python 3.4.2 Shell
File  Edit  Shell  Debug  Options  Windows  Help
Python 3.4.2 (v3.4.2:ab2c023a9432, Oct  6 201
C v.1600 32 bit (Intel)] on win32
Type "copyright", "credits" or "license()" fo
on.
>>> =============================== RESTART
================
>>>
Hello and welcome.
What is your name? Claire
It is great to meet you  Claire
>>>
```

4

Go back to the *Code* window and press `Enter`. Type in **colour=input('Tell me, what is your favourite colour?')**.

```
*Questions.py - C:/Python34/Questions.py (3.4.2)*
File  Edit  Format  Run  Options  Windows  Help
print('Hello and welcome.')
name=input('What is your name?')
print('It is great to meet you',name)
colour=input('Tell me, what is your favourite colour?')
```

5

Press `Enter` and type in **print('That is odd. I also like the colour', colour)**.

```
*Questions.py - C:/Python34/Questions.py (3.4.2)*
File  Edit  Format  Run  Options  Windows  Help
print('Hello and welcome.')
name=input('What is your name?')
print('It is great to meet you',name)
colour=input('Tell me, what is your favourite colour?')
print('That is odd. I also like the colour', colour)
```

6

Let's add a pause between the rest of the statements and questions. Press `Enter`. Type in **import time**, to import the time module, which is needed to use the sleep command. Press `Enter`. Type in **time.sleep(2)**. This runs the sleep command from the time module you just imported. This will pause the program for two seconds before moving on to the next command.

```
*Questions.py - C:/Python34/Questions.py (3.4.2)*
File  Edit  Format  Run  Options  Windows  Help
print('Hello and welcome.')
name=input('What is your name?')
print('It is great to meet you',name)
colour=input('Tell me, what is your favourite colour?')
print('That is odd. I also like the colour', colour)
import time
time.sleep(2)
```

7

Press `Enter` and type in **print('I need you to help me find my', colour, 'socks.')**.

Remember where it says *colour*, it will display the colour the user entered when asked about their favourite colour. This is another example of a variable.

```
*Questions.py - C:/Python34/Questions.py (3.4.2)*
File  Edit  Format  Run  Options  Windows  Help
print('Hello and welcome.')
name=input('What is your name?')
print('It is great to meet you',name)
colour=input('Tell me, what is your favourite colour?')
print('That is odd. I also like the colour', colour)
import time
time.sleep(2)
print('I need you to help me find my',colour,'socks.')
```

8

On the next line, type in **time.sleep(1)**. What do you think this command will do? Whatever number you put in the brackets will be the number of seconds the program pauses for.

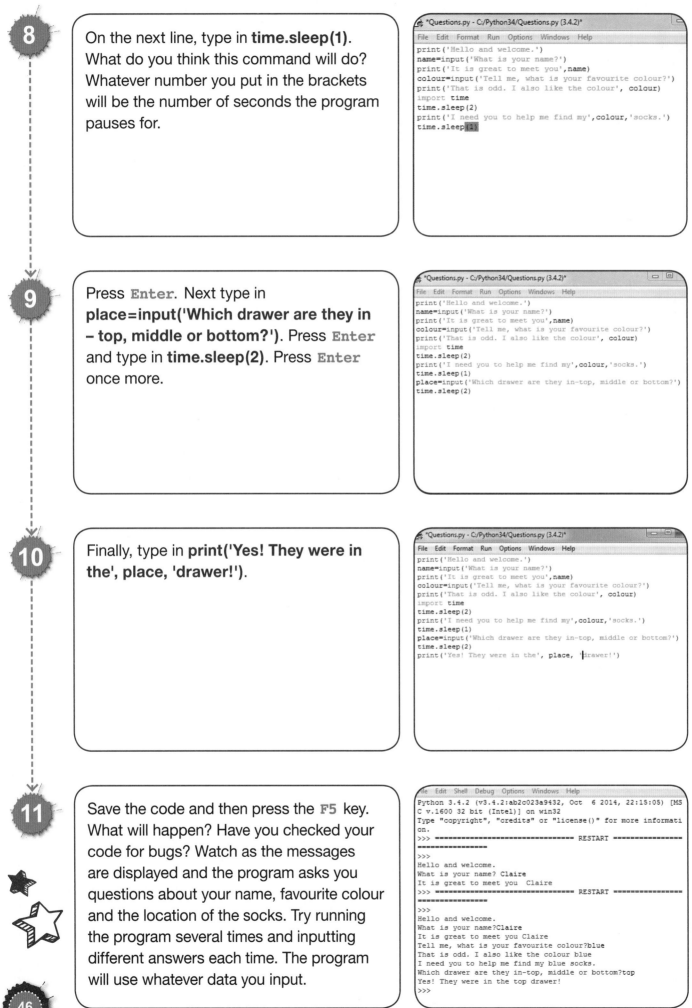

```
*Questions.py - C:/Python34/Questions.py (3.4.2)*
File  Edit  Format  Run  Options  Windows  Help
print('Hello and welcome.')
name=input('What is your name?')
print('It is great to meet you',name)
colour=input('Tell me, what is your favourite colour?')
print('That is odd. I also like the colour', colour)
import time
time.sleep(2)
print('I need you to help me find my',colour,'socks.')
time.sleep(1)
```

9

Press **Enter**. Next type in **place=input('Which drawer are they in – top, middle or bottom?')**. Press **Enter** and type in **time.sleep(2)**. Press **Enter** once more.

```
*Questions.py - C:/Python34/Questions.py (3.4.2)*
File  Edit  Format  Run  Options  Windows  Help
print('Hello and welcome.')
name=input('What is your name?')
print('It is great to meet you',name)
colour=input('Tell me, what is your favourite colour?')
print('That is odd. I also like the colour', colour)
import time
time.sleep(2)
print('I need you to help me find my',colour,'socks.')
time.sleep(1)
place=input('Which drawer are they in-top, middle or bottom?')
time.sleep(2)
```

10

Finally, type in **print('Yes! They were in the', place, 'drawer!')**.

```
*Questions.py - C:/Python34/Questions.py (3.4.2)*
File  Edit  Format  Run  Options  Windows  Help
print('Hello and welcome.')
name=input('What is your name?')
print('It is great to meet you',name)
colour=input('Tell me, what is your favourite colour?')
print('That is odd. I also like the colour', colour)
import time
time.sleep(2)
print('I need you to help me find my',colour,'socks.')
time.sleep(1)
place=input('Which drawer are they in-top, middle or bottom?')
time.sleep(2)
print('Yes! They were in the', place, 'drawer!')
```

11

Save the code and then press the **F5** key. What will happen? Have you checked your code for bugs? Watch as the messages are displayed and the program asks you questions about your name, favourite colour and the location of the socks. Try running the program several times and inputting different answers each time. The program will use whatever data you input.

```
File  Edit  Shell  Debug  Options  Windows  Help
Python 3.4.2 (v3.4.2:ab2c023a9432, Oct  6 2014, 22:15:05) [MS
C v.1600 32 bit (Intel)] on win32
Type "copyright", "credits" or "license()" for more informati
on.
>>> ============================= RESTART ================
================
>>>
Hello and welcome.
What is your name? Claire
It is great to meet you  Claire
>>> ============================= RESTART ================
================
>>>
Hello and welcome.
What is your name?Claire
It is great to meet you Claire
Tell me, what is your favourite colour?blue
That is odd. I also like the colour blue
I need you to help me find my blue socks.
Which drawer are they in-top, middle or bottom?top
Yes! They were in the top drawer!
>>>
```

Now try this . . .

- Can you add in a question that asks the user their age?

- Can you add in a response to the age question that says 'I am xx age too!'?

- Can you add in time delays between each message and question so they don't appear too quickly?

- Can you create your own scenario where you need the user to help you find a lost item?

Create a series of questions and responses about yourself and then muddle them up. Swap with a partner and try to match the responses to the correct questions.

Key words

Can you explain to a partner what these words mean?

program **code** **run** **input** **variable**

How did you do?

Think about what you did in this activity. Did you:

- create a program that asks a user to input information that the program uses later?

- add in another question for the user about their age?

- add in the correct code as a response to the user's answer about their age?

- add in the correct code so there are time delays between each message or question?

- create your own questions and answers scenario and code it as a program?

Activity 11: Python Random variables

In the previous activity, you used variables to store information the user typed in. Random variables allow a program to choose from a list of possible options. This activity uses random variables to create a program that simulates throwing a dice. This means the program will copy what happens when a real dice is thrown.

1 Start by opening IDLE. Click on `File` and then `New File` to open the code window. Type in **import random**. Using the random module will help us recreate the random nature of rolling a dice. The program will choose a number between 1 and 6.

```
*Untitled*
File  Edit  Format  Run  Options  Windows  Help
import random
```

2 Press `Enter`. Then type **import time**. This will enable us to put time delays in the program when it runs. Using these imported modules, such as the random and time modules, allows us to do more in Python.

```
*Untitled*
File  Edit  Format  Run  Options  Windows  Help
import random
import time
```

3 Press `Enter`. Now type in **min=1**. The minimum variable enables us to set the lowest number that can be 'thrown' on our virtual dice. In this case, the lowest number we want to be able to 'throw' on our virtual dice is 1.

```
*Untitled*
File  Edit  Format  Run  Options  Windows  Help
import random
import time
min=1
```

4 Press **Enter**. Then type in **max=6**. The maximum variable lets us set the highest number that can be 'thrown' on our virtual dice.

```
*Untitled*
File  Edit  Format  Run  Options  Windows  Help
import random
import time
min=1
max=6
```

5 Press **Enter** again and then type **dice=random.randint(min,max)**. This is instructing the program to randomly choose a number between the minimum and maximum numbers we have set.

```
*Untitled*
File  Edit  Format  Run  Options  Windows  Help
import random
import time
min=1
max=6
dice=random.randint(min,max)
```

6 Press **Enter**. Type **print('Hello! I am a virtual dice')**. Press **Enter** again. Type **time.sleep(1)**.

```
*Untitled*
File  Edit  Format  Run  Options  Windows  Help
import random
import time
min=1
max=6
dice=random.randint(min,max)
print('Hello! I am a virtual dice')
time.sleep(1)
```

7 Press **Enter** and type **print('The dice is rolling...')**.

```
*Untitled*
File  Edit  Format  Run  Options  Windows  Help
import random
import time
min=1
max=6
dice=random.randint(min,max)
print('Hello! I am a virtual dice')
time.sleep(1)
print('The dice is rolling...')
```

8

Press **Enter** and type in **time.sleep(3)**.

> We have increased the time delay here to build up to the score being revealed.

```
*Untitled*
File  Edit  Format  Run  Options  Windows  Help
import random
import time
min=1
max=6
dice=random.randint(min,max)
print('Hello! I am a virtual dice')
time.sleep(1)
print('The dice is rolling...')
time.sleep(3)
```

9

Finally, press **Enter** and type **print('You threw a...', dice, '!')**.

```
*Untitled*
File  Edit  Format  Run  Options  Windows  Help
import random
import time
min=1
max=6
dice=random.randint(min,max)
print('Hello! I am a virtual dice')
time.sleep(1)
print('The dice is rolling...')
time.sleep(3)
print('You threw a...', dice,'!')
```

10

It's time to test your virtual dice so save the code and then press **F5** to run the program. Try it several times and observe how the score changes randomly each time. Is this just like the result of throwing a real dice?

```
Python 3.4.2 Shell
File  Edit  Shell  Debug  Options  Windows  Help
Python 3.4.2 (v3.4.2:ab2c023a9432, Oct  6 2014,
on win32
Type "copyright", "credits" or "license()" for
>>> =============================== RESTART ==
>>>
Hello! I am a virtual dice
The dice is rolling...
You threw a... 5 !
>>>
```

Now try this . . .

- Can you change the maximum variable to simulate a 12-sided dice instead of a six-sided one?

- Can you increase the time delay before the score appears?

- Can you add the code for a second dice called *dice2* to simulate two dice being thrown at once?

- Can you add the command (*dice* + *dice2*) to calculate the total of the two dice throws?

- Compare using a virtual dice with using a real one – what are the pros and cons? Can you think of other uses for random variables?

Key words

Can you explain to a partner what these words mean?

variable   **minimum**   **maximum**   **program**   **random**

How did you do?

Think about what you did in this activity. Did you:

- create a program that simulates throwing a dice?

- change the code to simulate a 12-sided dice?

- increase the time before the score is revealed?

- add the code for a second random dice throw?

- create the code to add the scores from two random dice throws?

Activity 12: Python Combining different functions

You have explored using print, repetition and variables in Python. These can all be combined to create programs that do different things. The steps below show how to use them to create a story generator. This is a program that will randomly pick different elements of a story for you.

1 Start by opening IDLE. Click on `File` and then `New File` to open the *Code* window. Type in **import random** and press `Enter`. Then type in **import time**.

Remember that importing these modules allows us to program using time as random variables.

```
*Untitled*
File Edit Format Run Options Windows Help
import random
import time
```

2 Press `Enter` and type in **print('Stuck for ideas? Do not fear–I am the story generator!')**. Press `Enter` and type in **time.sleep(1)**.

```
*Untitled*
File Edit Format Run Options Windows Help
import random
import time
print('Stuck for ideas? Do not fear-I am the story generator!')
time.sleep(1)
```

3 Press `Enter` again. Type in **main=input('What would you like your main character to be called?')**. Press `Enter` and type **print('OK,', main, 'sounds good!')**. On the next line, type in **time.sleep(1)** again. This sets a variable called 'main'. It will change depending on what the user types in.

```
*Untitled*
File Edit Format Run Options Windows Help
import random
import time
print('Stuck for ideas? Do not fear-I am the story generator!')
time.sleep(1)
main=input('What would you like your main character to be called?')
print('OK,',main,'sounds good!')
time.sleep(1)
```

4

After that, press `Enter` again. Type **print('Your hero is...')**. Press `Enter` and type in **time.sleep(2)**. Press `Enter` once more.

```
*Untitled*
File  Edit  Format  Run  Options  Windows  Help
import random
import time
print('Stuck for ideas? Do not fear-I am the story generator!')
time.sleep(1)
main=input('What would you like your main character to be called?')
print('OK,',main,'sounds good!')
time.sleep(1)
print('Your hero is...')
time.sleep(2)
```

5

Now it's time to create some options for the hero of the story. Type in **goodie=['a dashing prince',** and press `Enter`. Type **'a brave and fearless penguin',** and press `Enter`. Type **'a wise owl']**. Press `Enter` again and type **print(random.choice(goodie))**.

> Each time the program runs it will pick one of these three heroes randomly.

```
*Untitled*
File  Edit  Format  Run  Options  Windows  Help
import random
import time
print('Stuck for ideas? Do not fear-I am the story generator!')
time.sleep(1)
main=input('What would you like your main character to be called?')
print('OK,',main,'sounds good!')
time.sleep(1)
print('Your hero is...')
time.sleep(2)
goodie=['a dashing prince',
        'a brave and fearless penguin',
        'a wise owl']
print(random.choice(goodie))
```

6

Press `Enter` and type **time.sleep(1)**. Press `Enter`. Type **print('The villain of your story is...')**. Press `Enter` again and type **time.sleep(2)**. Press `Enter` and type **baddie=['a wicked witch',** and press `Enter` again. Type **'a silent snake',** and press `Enter`. Now type **'a jealous emperor']**. Press `Enter` again and type **print(random.choice(baddie))**.

```
*Untitled*
File  Edit  Format  Run  Options  Windows  Help
import random
import time
print('Stuck for ideas? Do not fear-I am the story generator!')
time.sleep(1)
main=input('What would you like your main character to be called?')
print('OK,',main,'sounds good!')
time.sleep(1)
print('Your hero is...')
time.sleep(2)
goodie=['a dashing prince',
        'a brave and fearless penguin',
        'a wise owl']
print(random.choice(goodie))
time.sleep(1)
print('The villain of your story is...')
time.sleep(2)
baddie=['a wicked witch',
        'a silent snake',
        'a jealous emperor']
print(random.choice(baddie))
```

7

Press `Enter`. Type **time.sleep(2)**. Press `Enter` and type **print('And now it is time for the setting.')**. Press `Enter`. Type **time.sleep(1)**. Press `Enter`, then type **print('Your story will take place in...')**. Press `Enter`. Type **time.sleep(2)**.

```
*Untitled*
File  Edit  Format  Run  Options  Windows  Help
import random
import time
print('Stuck for ideas? Do not fear-I am the story generator!')
time.sleep(1)
main=input('What would you like your main character to be called?')
print('OK,',main,'sounds good!')
time.sleep(1)
print('Your hero is...')
time.sleep(2)
goodie=['a dashing prince',
        'a brave and fearless penguin',
        'a wise owl']
print(random.choice(goodie))
time.sleep(1)
print('The villain of your story is...')
time.sleep(2)
baddie=['a wicked witch',
        'a silent snake',
        'a jealous emperor']
print(random.choice(baddie))
time.sleep(2)
print('And now it is time for the setting.')
time.sleep(1)
print('Your story will take place in...')
time.sleep(2)
```

8

On a new line, type **location=['Central Park in New York',** and press **Enter**. Then type **'a quiet corner of the Sahara Desert',** and press **Enter**. Now type **'a haunted school']** and press **Enter** again. Type **print(random.choice(location))** and press **Enter**.

```
*Untitled*
File Edit Format Run Options Windows Help
import random
import time
print('Stuck for ideas? Do not fear-I am the story generator!')
time.sleep(1)
main=input('What would you like your main character to be called?')
print('OK, ',main,'sounds good'')
time.sleep(1)
print('Your hero is...')
time.sleep(2)
goodie=['a dashing prince',
        'a brave and fearless penguin',
        'a wise owl']
print(random.choice(goodie))
time.sleep(1)
print('The villain of your story is...')
time.sleep(2)
baddie=['a wicked witch',
        'a silent snake',
        'a jealous emperor']
print(random.choice(baddie))
time.sleep(2)
print('And now it is time for the setting.')
time.sleep(1)
print('Your story will take place in...')
time.sleep(2)
location=['Central Park in New York City',
          'a quiet corner of the Sahara Desert',
          'a haunted school']
print(random.choice(location))
```

9

Type **time.sleep(1)** and press **Enter**. Finally, type **print('and there you have the basis of your story!')**.

```
*Untitled*
File Edit Format Run Options Windows Help
import random
import time
print('Stuck for ideas? Do not fear-I am the story generator!')
time.sleep(1)
main=input('What would you like your main character to be called?')
print('OK, ',main,'sounds good'')
time.sleep(1)
print('Your hero is...')
time.sleep(2)
goodie=['a dashing prince',
        'a brave and fearless penguin',
        'a wise owl']
print(random.choice(goodie))
time.sleep(1)
print('The villain of your story is...')
time.sleep(2)
baddie=['a wicked witch',
        'a silent snake',
        'a jealous emperor']
print(random.choice(baddie))
time.sleep(2)
print('And now it is time for the setting.')
time.sleep(1)
print('Your story will take place in...')
time.sleep(2)
location=['Central Park in New York City',
          'a quiet corner of the Sahara Desert',
          'a haunted school']
print(random.choice(location))
time.sleep(1)
print('And there you have the basis of your story!')
```

10

Now it's time to test your story generator so save the code and press **F5** to run the program. Enter your name and then watch how the generator randomly picks a hero, villain and setting for you. Test it several times so you can see the random function in action.

```
Python 3.4.2 Shell
File Edit Shell Debug Options Windows Help
Python 3.4.2 (v3.4.2:ab2c023a9432, Oct  6 2014, 22:15:05) [MSC v.1600 32 bit (In
Type "copyright", "credits" or "license()" for more information.
>>> ================================ RESTART ================================
>>>
Stuck for ideas? Do not fear-I am the story generator!
What would you like your main character to be called?Sarah
OK, Sarah sounds good!
Your hero is...
a brave and fearless penguin
The villain of your story is...
a wicked witch
And now it is time for the setting.
Your story will take place in...
Central Park in New York City
And there you have the basis of your story!
>>>
```

Now try this . . .

○ Can you add in a fourth option for a hero?

○ Can you add a fourth villain?

○ Can you add in another location setting for the program to randomly choose from?

○ Can you add in another variable to go with the hero, villain and setting, such as the main character's friend or opening line?

Create different options for a hero, villain and setting of a story and randomly pick them out of a hat to create the basis for a story. What are the advantages and disadvantages of doing it digitally compared with this?

Key words

Can you explain to a partner what these words mean?

list   **variable**   **program**   **input**

How did you do?

Think about what you did in this activity. Did you:

○ create a program that generates a random story?

○ change the code to add another hero?

○ change the code to add another villain?

○ add a fourth location choice?

○ add another variable such as a randomly chosen friend or opening line?

Glossary

- **Accelerometer** [in App Inventor]: a sensor within an (Android) device that detects movement, e.g. if the device is tilted or shaken.

- **App:** a program or piece of software designed to meet a specific need – can be made for a variety of different operating systems (e.g. iOS, Android, Windows, etc.).

- **Block** [in App Inventor]: a section of code that has been grouped together to perform a specific action.

- **Button:** a graphic (image) used to provide a simple way to control when an event happens.

- **Code:** the sequence of commands or program you write using a programming language.

- **Command:** an instruction given to an object or character to make something happen.

- **Concatenate:** to arrange or join a series (string) of characters together.

- **Debug:** to find and get rid of errors within code.

- **Emulator:** a piece of software (or hardware) that duplicates the functions of one computer system within another – e.g. running Android software within a desktop computer environment.

- **For ... do loop** [in TouchDevelop]: repeat code a number of times.

- **Input:** information given to a computer to make something happen (e.g. a number, a mouse click or button press).

- **Interface:** a program that allows a user to communicate with a computer or a device.

- **Interpreter:** a computer program that follows instructions written in a programming language without converting them from source code.

- **Label:** a sequence of characters used to identify a location within code.

- **List:** a series of connected items.

- **Loop:** a statement that allows code to be continually (repeatedly) executed or performed.

- **Maximum:** the greatest amount that is allowed.

- **Minimum:** the smallest amount that is allowed.

- **Output:** something that a computer produces when given an instruction, e.g. a number, an on-screen image, a sound or vibration.

- **Pixel:** a tiny area of a display screen; a screen contains thousands of pixels, which are lit to form images.

- **Print:** a command used to display text on a screen.

- **Program:**
  1. a sequence of instructions written to perform a task or solve a problem, using a programming language (noun)
  2. to create or change a program (verb).

- **Random:** not in a particular order.

- **Repeat:** take a command (or set of commands) and follow its instruction again (and again).

- **Repetition:** the act of repeating something: following an instruction again (and again).

- **Run:** a command used to directly open a program.

- **Script:** a set of commands that are followed by a program.

- **Select:** to choose something.

- **Selection:**
  1. the act of selecting something
  2. one thing or a group of things that have been selected.

- **Sequence:** a set of commands that are performed one after another.

- **Simulate:** ask a computer to produce a 'model' of something happening, without actually having to do it.

- **Sprite:** an object or character that can be programmed.

- **String:** a sequence of characters, words or other data.

- **Text-to-speech:** a system that changes written text into a spoken voice.

- **Turtle:** the sprite used to draw a line in TouchDevelop.

- **Upload:** to transfer data from a computer (or device) to another source – this could be another computer, for example.

- **Variable:** a piece of data that changes or can be changed.

- **Wall:** the screen or interface used in the TouchDevelop programming tool.